Far-Fetched Pets

YOUR PET GIRAFFE

By Bobbie Hamsa

Illustrations by Tom Dunnington

Consultant:
James P. Rowan
Small Mammal House
Lincoln Park Zoo, Chicago

CHILDRENS PRESS, CHICAGO

For all the Eisenharts

CAUTION
Far-fetched pets can live only in your imagination. So don't ask for one for your birthday or Christmas. Go to the zoo or visit the library. There you can learn more about your favorite far-fetched pet.

Library of Congress Cataloging in Publication Data

Hamsa, Bobbie
Your pet giraffe.

(Far-fetched pets)
Summary: Lists the many pleasures of having a giraffe for a pet, including his abilities to get hay out of a hayloft, pick fruits you can't reach, and spot good places for a picnic a mile away.
[1. Giraffes—Anecdotes, facetiae, satire, etc.]
I. Dunnington, Tom, ill. II. Title. III. Series.
PZ7.H1887Yof [E] 81-12253
ISBN 0-516-03365-7 AACR2

Printed in the United States of America.
1 2 3 4 5 6 7 8 9 10 R 91 90 89 88 87 86 85 84 83 82

This is a giraffe.
A Reticulated Giraffe.
Pretend that he is your pet.

He has a light brown body.
Reddish-brown blotches.
Lovely eyes with long, lush lashes.
Four long legs and two horns.
And a long neck that makes him the world's tallest creature.
What will you name your pet giraffe?

CARE AND FEEDING OF YOUR PET

At first, milk is all your pet will eat.

But that doesn't last for long.

Soon he'll be hungry for bushels of beans.

And piles of pea pod salad.
He'll put away wagons full of wild apricots,
several servings of acacia bush hash,

and still have room for a thick, mimosa malt!

(Thank heavens he eats only twice a day.

Or you wouldn't have time for school.)

Feed him breakfast.

And dinner.

For lunch, he'll chew his cud.

(This means he spits up his breakfast and chews it again—only this time a little slower.)

Don't put his food down on the floor.

It'll be hard for him to reach.

Instead, make him promise not to nibble the shingles.

Then ask Dad if he can eat off the roof.

You need only two things to groom a giraffe: a warm day and all the help you can get.

Borrow big buckets,
long brushes,
and oodles of soap.
Ladders for leaning,
tin snips for toenails,
and garden shears to trim his mangy mane.

WARNING:

No matter how disgustingly dirty he gets, never use spot remover.

He needs his spots to hide from enemies.

Besides, he'll feel naked without them.

If he's young, your giraffe is called a calf.

And he's only as tall as your dad.

But by the time you're ten or eleven or so, he'll be as tall as or taller than your house.

So if you live in a city apartment, make sure that it's a high rise.

Or else your neighbors upstairs will be in for a big surprise!

He needs a place with room to grow.

And hard ground underfoot.

Perhaps you could rent a gymnasium?

Or a nearby empty elevator shaft? If not, rip the ceilings out of your house.

And get rid of the wall-to-wall carpet.

Most people think giraffes don't make noise.

But most people have never lived with one.

So if he wakes you with a few coughs or grunts in the night, just remember: it's better than sleeping with Grandma.

If he coughs a lot, though, take him to the vet.

(The last thing you need is a grumpy giraffe with a sore throat six feet long.)

Your pet has many good friends at the zoo.

Ostriches, zebras, and gnus.

So take him to visit them once in a while—

but don't let him bring them home.

(No gnus is *bad* news for zoos.)

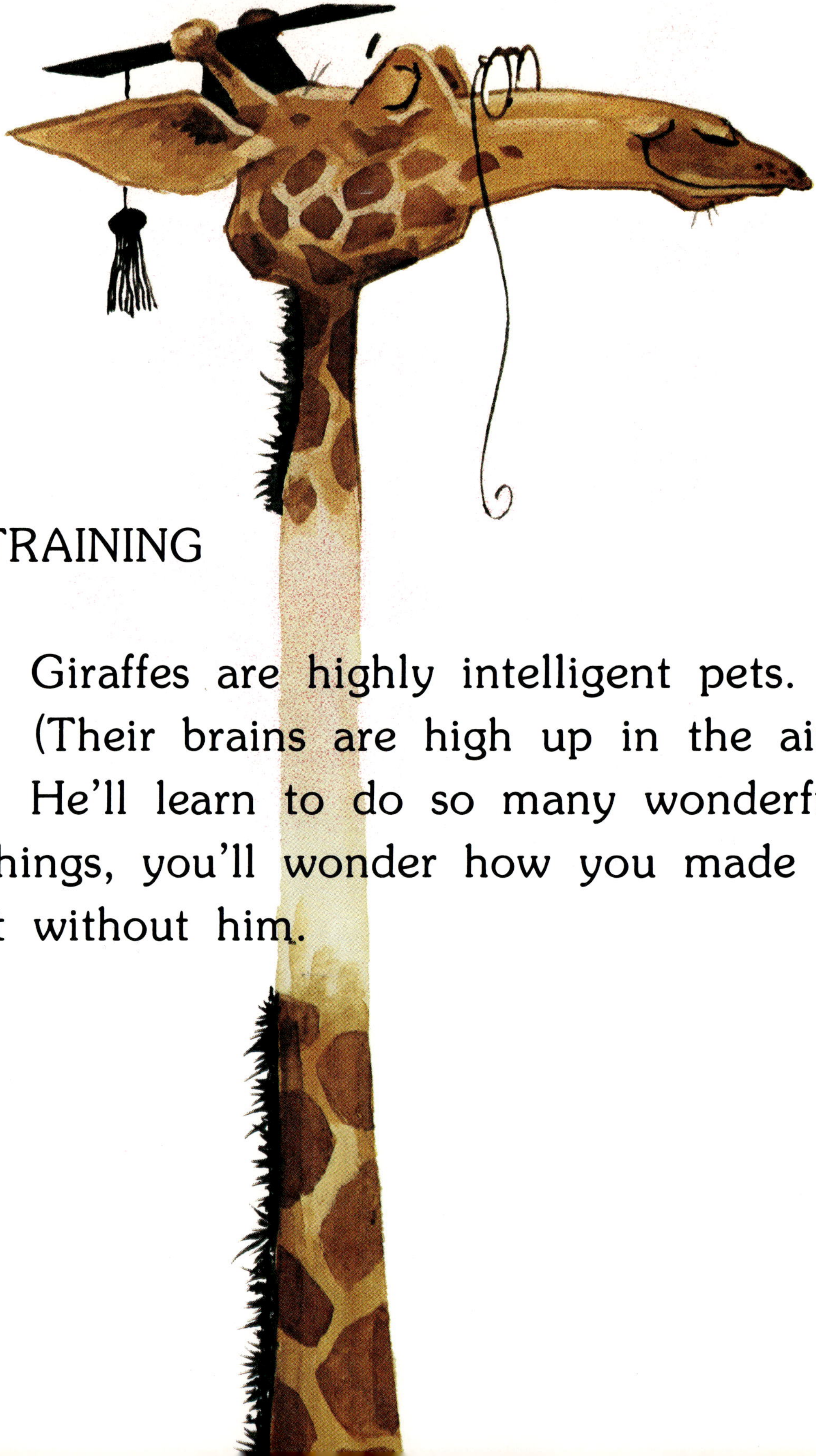

TRAINING

Giraffes are highly intelligent pets. (Their brains are high up in the air.) He'll learn to do so many wonderful things, you'll wonder how you made it without him.

He can carry you around on his neck to take aerial pictures of sand castles and such . . .

to spy on your brother while he plans April Fools . . .

and to peek at your parents when they're wrapping up presents and think you're safely in bed.

You can jump out of the house and slide down his neck when Mom calls for help with the dishes.

And if your sister ever threatens to run away, train him to run to the window and help her!

He can get hay out of Farmer Brown's hayloft and lift library books down from the shelves.

He can baby-sit squirrels while their mother's away . . . and he makes a fabulous bird feeder — (not the kind where birds come to the seed, but the kind where the seed comes to *them*).

If you go on a picnic, take him along.

He can spot a good spot a good mile away . . .
carry donuts and angel food cake
on his horns . . .
give Mom a quick lift if she
sees a snake . . .
and is he ever handy if you bump into a bull!

His tongue is black.

And as long as your arm.

He can grab things with it, too.

Let him clean leaves out of the gutters . . . and soot out of the chimney.

Let him pick cherries, apples, and nuts you can't reach . . . catch flies or flick them away.

Let him wash your face while you're still in bed (but make him gargle first).

Use him as a maypole in May . . .
a flag pole in June . . .
a bean pole in July . . .
a fishing pole in August . . .
and a telephone pole in an emergency.

These are only a few of the things your pet can do.

Can you think of more?

If you take good care of him, your giraffe will live maybe 20 years.

And you'll say he was the best pet you ever had.

Facts about your pet Reticulated Giraffe (Giraffa camelopardalis).

Size at birth (weight & height): about 6 feet in height, about 100 pounds in weight

Number of newborn: 1

Average size when grown (weight & height): up to 18 feet in height, up to 2000 pounds in weight

Type of food eaten: leaves and twigs of trees growing in African savannas, such as acacia

Amount of food eaten daily (not in captivity): a bushel or more

Expected lifespan: 20 to 25 years

Names—male: bull
female: cow
young: calf
group: herd

Where found: open savannas and dry acacia woodlands of East Africa

About the Author

Bobbie Hamsa was born and raised in Nebraska and has a Bachelor of Arts Degree in English Literature. She is an advertising copywriter for Bozell & Jacobs, Inc., writing print, radio, and television copy for many accounts, including "Mutual of Omaha's Wild Kingdom," the five-time Emmy Award winning wild animal series and sometime resource for Far-Fetched Pets. Bobbie lives in Omaha with her husband, Dick Sullivan, and children, John, Tracy, and Kenton.

About the Artist:

Tom Dunnington divides his time between book illustration and wildlife painting. He has done many books for Childrens Press, as well as working on textbooks, and is a regular contributor to "Highlights for Children." Tom lives in Oak Park, Illinois.